R.L.   5.1
Pts.   0.5

NO WAY

New Action Sports

Wrestling Basics

by Jeff Savage

CAPSTONE PRESS

MANKATO

C A P S T O N E   P R E S S

Capstone Press 818 Willow Street • Mankato, MN 55447

Library of Congress Cataloging-in-Publication Data
Savage, Jeff.
  Wrestling basics / Jeff Savage
    p. cm.
  Includes bibliographical references and index.
  Summary: An introduction to the history and basic techniques of wrestling.
  ISBN 1-56065-402-3
  1. Wrestling--Juvenile literature. [1. Wrestling.] I. Title.
GV1195.J395 1996
  796.8'12--dc20   95-44720
                                                            CIP
                                                            AC

Photo credits

USA Wrestling/Casey Gibson: pp. 4, 15, 41; Peter Widing: p. 38.
Archive Photos: pp. 6, 9, 19.
Peter Ford: pp. 10, 12, 13, 16, 20, 23, 24, 25, 27, 29, 30, 33, 34, 37, 46.

Table of Contents

Chapter 1 The History of Wrestling 5

Chapter 2 Pins, Points, and Rules 11

Chapter 3 Wrestling Equipment 17

Chapter 4 Safe Wrestling 21

Chapter 5 Wrestling Programs 35

Chapter 6 Great Wrestlers 39

Weight Classes.. 42

Glossary 44

To Learn More 46

Useful Addresses 47

Index 48

Words in **boldface** type in the text are defined in the Glossary in the back of the book.

Chapter 1

The History of Wrestling

W restling tests the strength, **stamina**, and skill of two opponents. Wrestlers come in all sizes. They compete against others of the same weight.

Wrestlers develop muscle strength, coordination, and confidence. No athlete works harder than a wrestler.

There have been wrestling champions since the Olympic games of 704 B.C.

European settlers brought wrestling to North America.

The Oldest Sport

Wrestling has been around a long time. We know from cave paintings that cave people used throws and strangles to defend themselves. Drawings of wrestlers have also been found on the walls of ancient tombs in Egypt.

Martial arts such as judo **evolved** from wrestling. Wrestling was a favorite activity of Native Americans. Wrestling is called the oldest sport.

Rome and Greece

Wrestling was popular in ancient Greece. It was introduced to the Olympic games in 704 B.C. Contestants wore brass knuckles with spikes. The winner was the wrestler who forced his opponent to touch the ground with any part of his body other than his feet.

The greatest Greek wrestler was Milo of Crotona. Milo won five Olympic **titles**. Legend says that Milo carried a calf around on his shoulders. As the calf got bigger, Milo's strength increased. Eventually, he was able to carry a full-grown ox on his back.

The Romans, who conquered Greece, developed a style of wrestling that is still used today. It is called **Greco-Roman** wrestling. In Greco-Roman wrestling, the legs cannot be used for attack or defense. Holds below the waist are not allowed.

Wrestling in North America

European settlers brought the Greco-Roman style of wrestling to the colonies in North America. The sport became popular in Vermont in the 1700s, where it was called collar and elbow.

During the U.S. Civil War (1861-1865), Union soldiers developed a new form of wrestling. They attacked from a standing position and used all parts of their bodies, including their legs. This wide-open style has become quite popular. It is called **freestyle** wrestling.

Greco-Roman and freestyle are still the two main types of wrestling. Both are used in international competition and in the Olympic games. They are also used in nearly all league, amateur, and non-school competitions in North America.

Two wrestlers grapple in the open air.

Folkstyle

School wrestling in the United States and Canada combines Greco-Roman and freestyle wrestling. This mixture of styles is called **folkstyle** wrestling. It is usually referred to as high-school wrestling or college wrestling.

International and Olympic wrestling feature faster action and more throws than folkstyle wrestling. The school style is based on control and holds.

Chapter 2
Pins, Points, and Rules

W restlers win when they **pin** their opponent or when they score more points than their opponent. A pin occurs when an opponent's back is turned to the mat and both shoulders are held firmly against it.

For a pin to occur in high-school wrestling, wrestlers must hold their opponents' shoulders against the mat for two seconds. In Greco-Roman and freestyle wrestling, the shoulders are held down for one second.

A near fall occurs when your opponent is threatened with a pin.

If there is no pin during a match, the person who scores the most points wins. Points are scored in four main ways.

A **takedown** is worth two points. It occurs when you take your opponent to the mat from a **neutral position**.

An **escape** is worth one point. An escape occurs when you slip free of your opponent's control.

A **reversal** is worth two points. It occurs when you take control from your opponent.

A reversal is worth two points.

Folkstyle wrestlers get points when they ride their opponents.

A **near fall** is worth either two or three points. A near fall occurs when your opponent is threatened for a pin. It is worth two points if your opponent's shoulders face the mat for two to four seconds. It is worth three points if your opponent's shoulders face the mat for five seconds or more.

Other Points

Folkstyle wrestlers are awarded one point for every minute they **ride** their opponents.

All wrestlers are warned once for using an illegal hold. They can also be warned for **stalling**. If they get two warnings, they are penalized one point.

Matches

The length of a wrestling match varies. Some freestyle and Greco-Roman contests last one five-minute period. College matches have a three-minute first period, followed by two periods that each last two minutes.

High-school matches usually consist of three periods that last two minutes each. Matches are shorter for younger wrestlers.

Wrestlers win when they pin their opponent. They can also win by scoring more points.

Chapter 3
Wrestling Equipment

W restling does not require much equipment. All a wrestler needs is a uniform, **head gear**, and a mat.

The Uniform

The standard wrestling uniform is called a **singlet**. It stretches from the shoulders to the thighs. It fits tight against the skin. The singlet's tight fit reduces the chance that wrestlers will grab each other's clothing, which is illegal. The singlet is made of a stretch fabric such as spandex.

The wrestling mat provides a cushion for the wrestlers.

The Head Gear

Two thin, fist-sized disks are the main components of a wrestler's head gear. The disks are made of hard plastic. They are sometimes lined with foam.

The disks cover the wrestler's ears. They are connected by plastic bands that wrap over the top of the head. An adjustable chin strap holds the head gear in place.

The head gear is sometimes called an ear guard. All college, high-school, and younger wrestlers must wear head gear. Head gear is not required in Olympic or international wrestling.

The Mat

The wrestling mat provides a cushion for the wrestlers' bodies. It is about one inch (2.5 centimeters) thick. It is made of foam wrapped with rubbery plastic. A circle is marked on the mat. Wrestlers must compete inside the circle.

Wrestling uniforms have changed throughout history.

Chapter 4

Safe Wrestling

All matches begin with both wrestlers on their feet in a neutral position. A good stance allows you to shoot forward or step back.

It is best to place one foot slightly forward. Spread your feet apart about shoulder-width. Bend your knees and crouch low. Keep your weight on the balls of your feet. Keep your eyes on your opponent.

Referee's Position

The second and third periods of high-school wrestling begin from the referee's position.

Right-handed wrestlers usually set up on the left side of the opponent.

This is a combination of two separate positions. They are the down position and the up position.

In the down position, you must be on your hands and knees. Your hands must be at least one foot (30 centimeters) in front of your knees. Lines on the mat guide the placement of your hands and knees. Keep your weight back and your hands pointed ahead. Your hands should rest lightly on the mat.

In the up position, you can be on either side of your opponent. Right-handed wrestlers usually set up on the left side of their opponents. Left-handed wrestlers usually set up on the right side.

Place your head over your opponent's back. Wrap one arm around his or her waist. Grip your opponent's elbow with your other hand.

At the start of the second period, the wrestler who is ahead chooses the position he or she wants to be in first. At the start of the third period, the wrestlers switch positions.

Arm takedowns are difficult.

Setups

When you set up a move from an upright stance, your goal is to get your opponent off-balance. Several combinations of fakes and grabs work well.

You can push on your opponent's chin to expose his leg, and then grab his leg. Or you can put one hand on the mat and fake toward one leg. Then grab the other leg.

You can push your opponent back with both hands to expose his or her legs. Then push one elbow up and grab both legs.

Remember, your opponent will be trying the same moves on you.

Takedowns

Once you have your opponent in a hold, you will want to score a takedown. There are several ways to do this.

The single-leg takedown is the most common. Shoot forward at your opponent's leg as you drop to one knee. Then grab the leg with

Single-leg takedowns are common.

It takes strength and speed to do a double-leg takedown.

both of your arms and pull it toward you. After your opponent falls to the mat, get on top of him or her.

A double-leg takedown is more effective, but it is difficult to do. It is nearly the same as the single-leg takedown, but you grab both of your opponent's legs instead of one.

Arm takedowns are difficult, too. They require more strength. An arm takedown is done by slipping underneath your opponent's arm, making a **crotch-lift** hold, and lifting your opponent up. Once you have your opponent up, take him or her down.

Another way to make an arm takedown is to grip your opponent's wrist, then pull him or her toward you, and duck your head under one arm. Then you will be able to slide behind your opponent and take him or her down.

If you are having trouble getting close enough to attempt a takedown, try an arm drag. Grab your opponent's wrist. Then quickly slide your other hand under one arm. Grip the upper arm. Then you will be able to control your opponent enough to attempt a takedown.

Lockups

When neither wrestler can score a takedown, they are in a lockup. You can then hand-and-arm wrestle to gain an advantage. To do this, grab your opponent behind the neck. Grip one arm behind the elbow with your other hand.

Then you can drop to your knees and take your opponent down by the legs.

Again, your opponent will try to counter each move.

The Wrestler's Grip

Once you have scored a takedown, you will need to control your opponent so he or she does not score an escape. A good way to hold your opponent is to use the wrestler's grip.

The wrestler's grip is almost impossible to break.

To make the grip, curl the fingers on both of your hands the way you would if you were hanging from an invisible rod. Hold your hands in front of your chest. Point one thumb up and the other thumb down.

Then **interlock** your hands. Curl your thumbs over your little fingers. When you wrap an opponent inside your arms and use the wrestler's grip, he or she will struggle to pry loose. But the opponent will not have much success. The wrestler's grip is nearly unbreakable.

Using Moves

After you have control of your opponent on the mat, you will want to get your opponent on his or her back. To do this, you will need to use a move, or several moves.

There are hundreds of moves and holds in wrestling. Learning all of them would take years. Newcomers should try to learn just a few. Then practice them over and over again.

There are hundreds of moves and holds in the sport of wrestling.

The best beginning wrestler is the one who knows a few moves very well. The wrestler who knows many moves but fails to do them properly will lose.

Popular Moves

The cradle, the guillotine, and the half nelson are three popular moves on the mat.

To do the cradle, bring your opponent's leg up to his or her head. Then reach behind your opponent's neck to form the wrestler's grip. To do the guillotine, wrap your legs around one of your opponent's legs. Then use the wrestler's grip behind your opponent's neck.

To do the half nelson, slip your arm under your opponent's arm and grip the back of his or her neck. When you do this move with both arms and hands it is called the full nelson. The full nelson is an illegal hold.

Winning Tips

Being aggressive is important. Do not fear your opponent or shy away. It is usually better to attack than defend. Be confident. Move swiftly. Be alert at all times. You can rest later.

If you lose a match, learn from it. Think about the moves you and your opponent made.

The best wrestlers are aggressive and confident.

Watch other matches. Good wrestlers will take the time to observe the competition. Be a student of wrestling.

Safe Conditioning

Wrestling is a physically demanding sport. Wrestlers must be in good physical condition. You get in good condition by exercising regularly and by eating the proper foods.

In the past, many wrestlers lost too much weight. They were even encouraged to do so by some coaches. Many wrestlers would not eat anything for several days before a match. Still, they practiced hard and wore many layers of clothes. This made them sweat a lot.

The more the wrestlers sweated, the more weight they lost. Some wrestlers lost 20 pounds or more between the start of the season and their first match.

These wrestlers were starving themselves. They thought they would wrestle better if they weighed less. Instead, they became weaker from the lack of nutritious food.

The best beginning wrestler is one who knows a few moves very well.

Sometimes the wrestlers got sick. Some had to be hospitalized. Eventually, people understood that a huge weight loss was not a good idea. Now, most coaches check their wrestlers' body fat. If a wrestler does not have enough body fat, he or she is not allowed to wrestle.

All wrestlers should have a physical examination before they wrestle.

Chapter 5

Wrestling Programs

W restling continues to attract more and more people. Programs are available to people of all ages through schools, clubs, churches, and other organizations.

Amateur Tournaments

Governing bodies such as United States of America Wrestling (USA Wrestling) and the Amateur Athletic Union (AAU) sponsor tournaments in the United States and Canada. Thousands of youngsters compete in regional tournaments each year.

Wrestlers struggle for position on the mat.

In 1995, the Northern Plains Regionals in La Crosse, Wisconsin, drew more than 1,000 wrestlers from eight states. The Western Regionals in California attracted 1,300 wrestlers from 12 states.

The Junior Nationals are held each year in Cedar Falls, Iowa. More than 2,000 boys and girls participate.

International Events

The best young wrestlers can compete for a world title in the Espoir World Championships, the Junior World Wrestling Championships, or the University World Games. Different cities host these events each year. The competitions attract worldwide attention.

School Wrestling

With high-school competition becoming more popular every year, junior high schools are forming teams to give young wrestlers a head start. Some elementary schools even conduct classes for children in fifth and sixth grades.

High-school wrestling is becoming more popular every year.

College Wrestling

Collegiate wrestling is popular, especially in the Midwest. The first National Collegiate Athletic Association (NCAA) wrestling tournament was held in 1928, in Ames, Iowa. For the next 57 years, a team from Iowa or Oklahoma won the NCAA title every year but three.

The World Championship of Women's Wrestling began in 1989. It is held each year in a different city.

Chapter 6

Great Wrestlers

Great wrestlers have come from many different countries. Abraham Lincoln, one of the greatest U.S. presidents, was known for his wrestling skills. Russia's George Hackenschmidt was undefeated in more than 400 matches. He was known as the Russian Lion. In 1908, Hackenschmidt was defeated by an Iowa farm boy named Frank Gotch.

Russia's Aleksandr Medved dominated the heavyweight division in international and Olympic competition through the 1960s. Japan's Osamu Watanabe won an Olympic gold

Today's champion wrestlers are smart as well as strong.

medal in the featherweight class in 1964 with his 186th straight victory.

Hall of Fame

In 1976, the National Wrestling Hall of Fame and Museum opened in Stillwater, Oklahoma. A Wall of Champions at the Hall of Fame features the names of more than 5,000 wrestlers.

George Washington, Abraham Lincoln, and Theodore Roosevelt are three famous U.S. presidents honored in the hall. Boys as young as 10 years old are honored, too, as are many girls and women.

Dan Gable and Wayne Wells are also honored. They each won a gold medal in the 1972 Olympics. They were the first Americans to win gold medals in Olympic wrestling.

Gable has won nearly every tournament available to a wrestler. He won 100 matches in a row when he wrestled at Iowa State University. He went on to coach the University of Iowa wrestling team to nine straight NCAA titles.

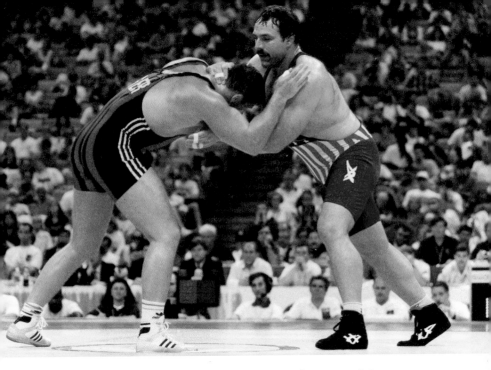

Bruce Baumgartner (right) is a three-time world champion.

Strong into the Future

Basic wrestling rules and equipment have not changed much through the years.

Coaches and athletes, though, have constantly worked to improve their chances of winning. They have created new moves, holds, and drills. Today's wrestlers are better skilled than wrestlers of the past.

The oldest sport remains one of the strongest sports.

Weight Classes

Here are the weight classes for three levels of wrestling competition.

High-School Wrestling
103 pounds (46.4 kilograms)
112 pounds (50.4 kilograms)
119 pounds (53.6 kilograms)
125 pounds (56.3 kilograms)
130 pounds (58.5 kilograms)
135 pounds (60.8 kilograms)
140 pounds (63 kilograms)
145 pounds (65.3 kilograms)
152 pounds (68.4 kilograms)
160 pounds (72 kilograms)
171 pounds (77 kilograms)
189 pounds (85.1 kilograms)
275 pounds (123.8 kilograms)

College Wrestling

118 pounds (53.1 kilograms)

126 pounds (56.7 kilograms)

134 pounds (60.3 kilograms)

142 pounds (64 kilograms)

150 pounds (67.5 kilograms)

158 pounds (71.1 kilograms)

167 pounds (75.2 kilograms)

177 pounds (79.7 kilograms)

190 pounds (85.5 kilograms)

177-275 pounds (79.7-123.8 kilograms)

Olympic and International Wrestling

105.5 pounds (47.5 kilograms)

114.5 pounds (51.5 kilograms)

125.5 pounds (56.5 kilograms)

136.5 pounds (61.4 kilograms)

149.5 pounds (67.3 kilograms)

163 pounds (73.4 kilograms)

180.5 pounds (81.2 kilograms)

198 pounds (89.1 kilograms)

220 pounds (99 kilograms)

over 220 pounds (over 99 kilograms)

Glossary

crotch lift—a move in which the wrestler uses one arm through the crotch and one arm around the leg to take down his opponent

escape—a move in which the wrestler slips free of his opponent's control

evolve—when something develops over a long time with gradual changes

folkstyle—a blend of freestyle and Greco-Roman forms of wrestling. Folkstyle is primarily used in high-school competition.

freestyle—a wide-open form of wrestling in which wrestlers attack from the standing position and use all parts of the body

Greco-Roman—a form of wrestling in which legs cannot be used for attack or defense. Holds below the waist are not allowed.

head gear—a piece of equipment that covers and protects the ears

interlock—to join together

near fall—situation in which a wrestler is threatened for a pin

neutral position—situation in which both wrestlers are on their feet and not engaged

pin—a move in which the wrestler's shoulders are held firmly against the mat for a specific time

reversal—a move in which control is switched from one wrestler to the other

ride—when a wrestler controls his opponent by holding at least one leg and one arm

singlet—the uniform worn by most wrestlers in competition

stalling—circumstance in which a wrestler avoids or delays action

stamina—the power to resist getting tired while working hard

takedown—a move in which the wrestler is forced to the mat by his opponent

title—an award given to the champion of a sport

To Learn More

Clayton, Thompson. *An Introduction to Wrestling.* New York: A.S. Barnes and Co., 1970.

Gutman, Bill. *Sumo Wrestling.* Minneapolis: Capstone Press, 1995.

Hopke, Stephen L. *Elementary and Junior High School Wrestling.* Cranbury, N.J.: A.S. Barnes and Co., 1977.

Valentine, Tom. *Inside Wrestling.* Chicago: Contemporary Books, 1972.

Useful Addresses

Amateur Athletic Union
3400 West 86th Street
P.O. Box 68207
Indianapolis, IN 46268

Canadian Olympic Association
Olympic House
2380 Avenue Pierre Dupuy
Cite du Havre
Montreal, PQ H3C 3R4
Canada

**National Wrestling Hall of Fame and
 Museum**
405 West Hall of Fame Avenue
Stillwater, OK 74075

USA Wrestling
6155 Lehman Drive
Colorado Springs, CO 80918

Index

Amateur Athletic Union, 35
Ames, Iowa, 37

collar and elbow, 8
cradle, 29, 31

Egypt, 6
escape, 12, 27
Espoir World Championships, 36

folkstyle, 9, 14
full nelson, 31

Gable, Dan, 40
Greco-Roman, 7, 8, 9, 11, 14
Greece, 7
Gotch, Frank, 39
guillotine, 29, 31

Hackenshmidt, George, 39

half nelson, 29, 31

Iowa State University, 40

judo, 7
Junior Nationals, 36

Lincoln, Abraham, 39, 40

Medved, Alexandr, 39
Milo of Crotona, 7

National Wrestling Hall of Fame, 40
NCAA, 37, 40
near fall, 13
neutral position, 12, 21

referee's position, 21

reversal, 12
Romans, 7

spandex, 17
Stillwater, Oklahoma, 40

University of Iowa, 40
University World Games, 36
USA Wrestling, 35

Washington, George, 40
Watanabe, Osamu, 39
Wells, Wayne, 40
World Championship of Women's Wrestling, 37
World Wrestling Championships, 36